MASTERING BUSINESS WRITING

Don't let fear or uncertainty of business writing skills hold you back from success: the fact is, most business schools do not focus on the importance of writing in the business world, and few companies offer formal training in the field.

For powerful communication in business every day, *Mastering Business Writing* is your key to success!

You'll learn the basics of good writing and helpful advice on:

- Hooking your readers
- The power of the written word
- Getting started
- Research
- Outlines
- The art of revision
- Dealing with writer's block
- Using a thesaurus
- Grammar, syntax, and punctuation
- Choosing a writing style
- Technical writing
- Reports
- Cover letters
- Resumes
  . . . AND MUCH MORE!

THE TOTAL MANAGEMENT PROGRAM FOR THE 1990s!
From the National Institute of Business Management

THIS REMARKABLE NEW SERIES INCLUDES:

MASTERING MEETINGS
MASTERING OFFICE POLITICS
MASTERING DECISION MAKING
MASTERING BUSINESS WRITING
MASTERING BUSINESS STYLE (Coming soon)

THE ESSENTIAL KEYS TO SUCCESS FOR
TODAY'S MANAGERS

MASTERING BUSINESS WRITING

The Executive's Guide to the
Essentials of Good Writing

NATIONAL INSTITUTE OF BUSINESS MANAGEMENT

Previously published under the
title *Power Business Writing*.

BERKLEY BOOKS, NEW YORK

This book was previously published under the title
Power Business Writing.

MASTERING BUSINESS WRITING

A Berkley Book / published by arrangement with
National Institute of Business Management, Inc.

PRINTING HISTORY
National Institute of Business Management, Inc. edition / September 1989
Berkley trade paperback edition / August 1991

ISBN: 0-425-12856-3

A BERKLEY BOOK ® TM 757,375
Berkley Books are published by The Berkley Publishing Group,
200 Madison Avenue, New York, New York 10016.
The name "BERKLEY" and the "B" logo
are trademarks belonging to Berkley Publishing Corporation.

PRINTED IN THE UNITED STATES OF AMERICA

10 9 8 7 6 5 4 3 2 1

CONTENTS

THE POWER
OF THE
WRITTEN WORD

Why write? We live in an audiovisual society, after all. Stenographers are in ample supply. We conduct much important business over the phone, over a conference table, over lunch. Why, then, must executives struggle with that mortal enemy, the written word?

The question, of course, is rhetorical. Writing remains essential to confirm verbal agreements, stipulate terms, and supply the detailed information needed for any major decision. Few managers will climb high without mastering the craft of business writing. Dictation will never replace the carefully planned, personally crafted letter. From job applications to annual corporate reports, we are measured by our sentences.

In a recent Hodge-Cronin survey of 800 chief executive officers, 98% agreed that writing ability was "important for success," both in their positions and other executive posts throughout their companies. "The ability to communicate is at the top of the promotability ladder," says John Fielden, a consultant and professor of management communication at the University of Alabama. Good writing will save the boss's time and create a positive impression. Poor writing will brand the writer as disorganized, tedious, even unreliable.

For executives, to write is to sell. To explain is not enough; you must *persuade*. Every message markets an idea, and must vie with scores of other messages in an increasingly crowded marketplace. Only the clearest and most persuasive communications are sure to be read.

Many cannot compete in this market. Eighty-three percent of the Hodge-Cronin CEOs found younger managers ill-trained in writing. The major complaints: wordiness; poor organization; inappropriate tone; no clearly stated purpose.

To their credit, executives are self-critical on this subject. In a Communispond survey, 53% rated their writing skills fair or poor, and 44% wanted to improve the clarity and organization of their documents. Tellingly, only 25% said they enjoyed writing, and 72% placed it at the top of their "hate list"—along with speaking and attending in-house business meetings.

Little wonder. Writing is given scant attention in business schools. Most companies offer little or no formal training—and few executives are natural writers by temperament. Their professional lives are fast-paced, interactive, and highly goal-oriented. Writing is a slow and solitary process with uncertain results.

The good news is that competent writers are made, not born. *Mastering Business Writing* will examine four major facets of *all* effective writing: clarity, brevity, style, and grammar. It will apply these principles to specific business forms, from reports and proposals to letters and memoranda. Finally, it will consider the *process* of writing, from research to revision—and how to overcome any stumbling blocks in between.

Business writers work under special conditions and pressures. They face rigid deadlines. They write for high stakes, whether to win a contract for their company or to enhance their professional reputation. They are rarely experts as they begin a writing project; they must grasp new subjects quickly, and move from one to the next without breaking stride. And they must juggle their writing with a dozen other daily tasks.

But at bottom, good business writing is good writing. To master their craft, as E.B. White once noted, all writers must love "the clear, the brief, the bold" and avoid "the vague, the tame, the colorless, the irresolute." As you already know, that prescription is easier said than done. Our aim is to help you in the doing.

HOOKING
YOUR READERS
(AND HAULING
THEM IN)

Writing has but one true test, and that is effectiveness. To be effective, you must know three things—your audience, your purpose, and what you want the former to do about the latter. If you hope to persuade and gain action, you must think all three elements through *before* you write.

Who are you writing for? Are they executives or technicians, experts or laymen? What do they know about the subject you're addressing? Do they know the field's jargon? What do they *need* to know? Do they have biases or expectations? Who is your *primary* reader, the one to take action? Is there a hidden audience which could help or hinder your objective?

After answering these questions, try to visualize your audience. If a memo is aimed at several executives, pick one—just as you would focus on a single face when giving a lecture. Hold a firm mental picture of your reader when you write. Think about how you'd talk to that person, and how your reader would respond. Consider the person's interests, concerns, and attitudes. Ask not, "What can I tell my reader?" but rather "How can my message be *useful* to this person?"

The answer will dictate your writing style, your tone of voice, the order of your ideas, and which points get more attention. But one element never varies. To be useful to your readers, your message must get to its point—and at once. What are you trying to achieve? Do you hope to inform or instruct, analyze or evaluate, persuade or provoke? What do you want to *change* in your reader's mind? What *action* are you aiming for? Are you seeking one-time approval, or continuing involvement in your project? Let your audience know, and don't make them wait.

Before you inform your readers, of course, you must mull over these matters for yourself. Many business-writers cheat themselves from the start; they don't invest enough time to *think* before they write. They pay for their hurry later on, with interest. Your *purpose* (and point of view) will determine what must be covered in depth, what may be touched on briefly, what may be skipped. Your *scope* will tailor the amount and direction of your research and the detail of your notes. Your *audience* will dictate both the order of your presentation and which terms must be explained. (In any case, remember that your readers are rarely as familiar with your subject as you are. Better to tell them something they know than to confuse by omission.) If you fail to resolve these issues before you write, you are doomed to wasted work and torturous revision. It is far easier to correct a blueprint than a concrete foundation, to revise a recipe than a finished stew. In sum, your most valuable writing time comes before you set pen to paper. Much of your best work may occur while you're in the shower or staring out a window.

To aid your preparation, segregate pure thinking from writing. If possible, work at two chairs; when you're in your "thinking" chair, you won't feel impelled to pick up a pen or touch your keyboard. If your workspace is limited, it may help to shift a single chair in different directions. (While you're ruminating, for example, you might face sideways. Then face front to write.)

UNLOCKING YOUR WRITING POWER

Maximum Research in Minimum Time

To gather information, writers often start with written sources, then fill in any gaps through interviews with experts. They neglect a prime source of guidance: themselves.

Between your formal education and business experience, you know more about most subjects than you're aware of. Many insights lie half-forgotten, just under the edge of memory. Others need new connections to the project at hand. Your task is to bring all your accumulated knowledge to the surface. It's time to brainstorm.

Start by simply jotting down ideas as they come, in any order. Don't impose a structure; forget about neatness and spelling. Let your mind freewheel. Write each idea on an index card. When your flow of new thoughts peters out, go back and list supporting details for each idea.

Later on, if you rearrange the cards, you'll have a tentative outline for your project. But that is secondary at this point. Brainstorming frees your brain to wander through old pastures and retrieve lost treasures of thought. The act feeds on itself; once you kick into gear, you'll find your pen racing to keep pace. For maximum benefit, perform this self-interview before any other research. Brainstorming will refine your purpose and point of view, and steer you to the right outside sources.

Most of those sources will be either in company files or libraries. Unless your subject is obscure or unusually narrow, you'll have no trouble finding enough background information. Between the card catalogue (for books) and *The Reader's Guide to Periodical Literature* (for magazines and journals), you'll collect more sources than you can use—and certainly more than you have time to read, cover-to-cover.

Professional writers routinely spend months on research for a story they'll write in a week or less. Business writers rarely have so much time. You must winnow out the chaff and decide which sources deserve your effort. Start by checking a book's index (or by skimming a magazine article), to make sure the source speaks to your needs. If you find material of value, it's time to take notes.

Note-taking is an art in itself. If you record more

than you need, your notes will waste your time twice—in the act of recording and later on, when you must search for the nugget of information you desire. But if you take down too little, you'll have to return to the original source while you're writing. That wastes even more time. With the right technique, however, your note-taking will be lean but sufficient:

- Never sacrifice clarity for brevity, especially in notes on abstract ideas. Pose a question: Will your notes enable you to recall the significant ideas a week later?
- Copy word-for-word only when you plan a direct quote from the source. Otherwise, paraphrase (and shorten) the author's point. By making small but constant changes from the text, you'll avoid inadvertent plagiarism—and help bridge to your writing phase.
- Confine your notes to primary ideas. You won't have room to write about the secondary or peripheral.
- Create your own shorthand. Delete vowels when possible, and use numerals rather than writing numbers out.
- Check all pertinent names, dates, and definitions for accuracy. Then double-check.
- Mark questionable notes with question marks, particularly when they contradict other sources.
- Make sure you can retrieve the source if neces-

sary. Note the title, author, date (for periodicals), and page numbers.

In some cases, you'll need to gather expert analysis or opinion through personal interviews. Whole books focus on interview technique; like most crafts, it resists easy mastery. Interviews are essentially similar to any casual business conversation. In either case, you extract specific information in a purposeful manner. But formal interviews involve an added layer of planning and artfulness:

- When you reach your experts (whether by letter or phone), begin by explaining who you are, the nature of your project, why you chose them, and the terrain you'd like to cover. Where time and protocol permit, offer to show them a draft of your work when completed. If they agree to be interviewed, set a convenient time.
- Before asking your first question, confirm the ground rules. An interview may either be off the record (for background), or on the record (for attribution). An off-the-record talk helps sources relax, since they know they won't be quoted by name. But if you're reporting on a new personnel plan, for example, your work will lack authority if it fails to quote (or paraphrase) the personnel manager. A compromise: Tell your sources you won't quote them *unless*

they authorize a specific attribution at your later request. Then proceed with your conversation as if it were off the record.

Compose a list of *specific* questions, in the order you plan to ask them, from most to least important. If you run out of time, you'll have covered the most critical points.

- Be courteous but bold. Don't shy away from pertinent questions, even if they seem delicate or embarrassing. If your sources don't like the question, they can always decline to answer.
- Your job is to draw out the interviewee and to *listen*. Keep your questions short and pointed; hold interjections to a minimum. Assume that your expert has no interest in your opinions.
- If an answer prompts a follow-up question, ask it right away. If you wait, you may forget to pursue it.
- When your source rambles off the subject, excuse yourself and interrupt with the next question on your list.
- Use a tape recorder only when you must have quotes word-for-word. (A one-hour talk can take two to three hours to transcribe.) Take notes as you go, but don't bury your head in your note pad. Eye contact encourages more open conversation—and allows the interviewer to maintain control.

- After concluding the interview, reconstruct it with notes or a tape recording. Don't delay. If you wait until the next day, you'll forget much of the detail.

Research can be seductive. As you become more expert on a given subject, you'll want to learn still more—for its own sake. Resist that temptation. Research, after all, is only a means to your end of *writing*. You can always check one more article, talk to one more person. But there comes a time when you must set all preparation aside and launch your project proper. To do otherwise is to procrastinate, to steal from valuable writing time. Set a deadline to end your research phase, and stick to it. You can fill any gaps later.

Outlines:
Your Key to Persuasive Structure

In a random study of 2,000 corporate reports, letters, and memos, only one in twenty were organized effectively. Most of these messages were mechanically correct. They used the proper words. But they failed to persuade because their arguments or analyses failed to proceed in a logical order. Rather than build to an irresistible conclusion, they meandered or petered out. They promised a tour by limousine, but delivered a midnight safari, full of unexpected bumps and swerves.

Writers can rescue their readers by planning their mutual journey ahead of time. For brief letters and memos, the plan may be simply a list of pertinent phrases, to ensure nothing important is left out. But for any communication longer than five pages, only an outline will do. And the more complex your subject (and the less secure you feel about it), the fuller your outline should be.

An outline packages your ideas in the most powerful sequence and filters out nonessentials. It ensures a balanced structure—a beginning, middle, and end—and emphasizes key points by planting them in prominent places. It reveals gaps in your research or logic—problems that would be tougher to correct in a finished draft. Not least, an outline takes much of the pain and paralysis out of writing. With a good outline as framework, writing a report is like filling in the colors of a pre-drawn canvas. Work your outline as you would a challenging puzzle, until you solve your subject. Every hour you spend may save you three in actual writing.

Mental outlines don't work. According to psychologist George A. Miller, people can retain only seven units of information at a time. You will need, therefore, either a set of index cards or a clean legal pad. Beyond that, there is no one way to outline. Writers eventually settle on a method that works for them and their subject matter. Here are four options:

- **The jot outline** consists of random notes recorded as thoughts occur or your research proceeds. Neatness and logic are low priorities at this stage. Jot outlines are ideal for writers with only a tentative sense of purpose. Before writing, of course, they have to develop a more complete, better-organized outline.
- **The topic outline** arranges material according to subject matter, using key words or sentence fragments as headings and subheadings. To get started, take several sheets of scratch paper and label the top of each with a key concept, or *general heading*. These concepts must be related but separate; if they overlap, they will muddy your plan.(For this report, general headings included, *Hooking Your Readers*, *Getting Started*, and *Clarity*.)
- Next, summarize and distribute your interview and book notes (and any other *pertinent* research) under the respective headings. Key each note with a page number to allow you to find it again.
- When you're finished, examine each scratch sheet and decide which points call for inclusion in your report or proposal. After that, it's a relatively simple job to transfer these points, in outline form, to your index cards or legal pads.

Again, use one general heading per card or page.

Major headings are traditionally ordered with Roman numerals. Subheadings, which support or qualify the main topics, use upper-case letters. Sections are numbered, and sub-sections use lower-case letters. (If you need more than four heading levels, your outline is *too* complex.) Each successive lower level is indented further to the right, to denote its relative importance.

- **The sentence outline** is a fleshed-out version of the topic outline. Your concepts and supporting evidence are translated into complete sentences, rather than fragments. Each sentence should be direct and specific. Your finished outline should parallel your final document—not only in order and logic, but also in the amount of space given to each element.

  A complete sentence outline is the best cure for so-called writer's block. No longer will you stop and agonize over what comes next. You'll *know* what comes next by glancing at your legal pad. What you have, in fact, is the core of a first draft. It requires only transitional sentences or phrases to become a bona fide report or proposal.

- **The organization tree** is a horizontal alternative to the traditional vertical outline. Turn your legal pad on its side and place the trunk of the tree—your central point, or purpose—on the far left of the page. The main branches—your primary arguments—run down the middle, and each is linked to smaller branches—supporting evidence—on the right side of the page. (Just as every branch is tied to its trunk, make sure that every point supports your purpose.)

The tree method makes it easier to add afterthoughts as you go along. Some writers also find the horizontal sketch more helpful visually. For best results, "branch" for at least 10 minutes. As in brainstorming, write down every idea that occurs to you, no matter how absurd. Forget about structure and form; let your pattern emerge from your material. An organizational tree can be a godsend for writers who feel smothered by more traditional, linear methods.

An outline is the greatest gift to business writers since the ballpoint pen. It can also become a counter productive infatuation. A straightjacket outline smothers inspiration and limits your message's potential. If you labor over every small detail and precise ordering, you defeat your goal—to make writing easier. Experienced writers leave themselves room for creativity in the writing process itself. They feel free to detour as they go along—

and may even discard an outline toward the end of their work, when all major points are accounted for.

First Sentences
That Really Count
with Readers

Journalists call it the *lead*—the opening sentence or paragraph in a story, the lure they use to grab their readers. Like all first impressions, that opening sentence is crucial. If it is clear and dynamic, a reader will forge on in a generous frame of mind. If it is muddled or dull, the same person will continue reluctantly or not at all.

Publishers say they can tell whether a novel will make it by reading the first ten pages. If the average reader isn't hooked by then, the book will be tossed aside. In business writing there is even less time to dawdle. Assume that your boss is always facing an emergency.

Unfortunately, much business writing reserves its purpose or conclusion for the close, like a punch line without the joke. Junior executives seldom see bluntness rewarded. They are loathe to lay their necks on *any* line, even when bearing good news. They view buried conclusions and circuitous logic as protective devices.

Ironically, top executives say they long for direct, straight-forward communication—like the memos they write themselves. The concealed punch line leaves them frustrated at best. At worst, it simply leaves them, its mumbled message unread.

The solution is simple: Don't start your business writing at the beginning. Start at the *ending*. State your conclusion and action-steps first—possibly in the first sentence of your executive (introductory) summary, probably within the first paragraph. Write like a reporter, with your "lead" at the top. A summary lead lends your purpose a motive, and gives your readers a frame of reference for the background to follow. Because they know what's coming, they need less time and strain to understand it. And by stating your purpose, you can better gauge the rest of your message: Are you addressing the problem (or solution) you posed? Most important, you will know when your writing is finished. When you've fulfilled your purpose, your job is done.

It is difficult to be *too* direct or obvious in this lead statement. As E.B. White observed, "When you say something, make sure you have said it. The chances of your having said it are only fair." (In a memo or brief letter, it's best to barge right in: "In your memo of June 17, you asked about the progress of . . .")

Not every lead has to be a blunt instrument, however. Too obvious an opening ("The purpose of this report is . . .") will annoy readers who prefer a touch of subtlety. A lead can be just as direct, and much more intriguing, when it both states and begins to *describe* its purpose, or promises a solution, or sets a dramatic stage: "Without new markets to penetrate, our division faces a 10 percent loss in revenues."

With a sophisticated audience, you can drop your lead to the second and third paragraphs of a long report or proposal. (For an example, check the beginning of this report.) In sensitive or negative situations, you may properly defer your lead even further—the "slow no" approach. Keep in mind, however, that very few communications demand this gentle handling.

While all leads share the same mission, they can do their duty in a wide variety of ways. Choose your lead format with an eye on the tone you hope to set, the readers you seek to reach, and the type of material to follow. Some options:

- State the problem you're addressing, or summarize the events which led up to the matter at hand. *Caution:* when readers are familiar with this background, this lead will bore them if it runs too long.
- Define a central concept, assuming that most of your readers need help with it. But avoid the stilted "Webster defines inventory as . . ."
- Use a revealing detail or anecdote. These leads

ingratiate, even entertain. Your readers will welcome them—especially if the following material is dense or technical. But don't get too windy; if a story rambles, your point will be lost.

- Try a quote—but only if it pertains to your topic and purpose. A catchy quote will only mislead your readers if it conflicts with your own conclusions or analysis.
- Predict the future in your subject area. A dramatic forecast is a great hook, as long as you are able to back it up in the body of your piece.
- Define the scope of your project. This lead works best in brief reports or proposals that lack an abstract or table of contents.

The Rough Draft—Without Agony

After grabbing your audience with a solid opening, you still have to keep them with you the rest of the way. To read a long report through is an act of faith. Your readers must trust that you have their best interests at heart, that you are objective (though not necessarily neutral), and that you won't desert them midway. You can reward their faith by following some basic principles of good writing. For example:

1. Treat your paragraphs like rungs on a ladder. Each should lead logically to the next. Bridge any gaps with transitional sentences. Some standard transitions: "At the same time, . . ."; "Even so, . . ."; "Here again. . . ."

2. Relate the unknown to something the reader already knows. When introducing an unusual or technical term, define it. The definition can follow the word in parentheses: "The debenture (bond) market offered a safe and moderate return." Or, more gracefully, it can be welded into the sentence: "Despite falling bond interest rates, the debenture market seemed a safe bet."

3. Long reports can grow monotonous, no matter how urgent the topic. To break a lulling rhythm, vary the length and structure of your sentences.

4. Remember that bare facts are not enough. The president of a New Jersey electronics lab once set about to improve employee relations. He decided to reduce daily working hours by one half-hour. He said as much—and only that much—in a memo to his staff. The response? Insecure workers feared future layoffs. A hostile employee spread the false rumor that lunch hour would be cut to 30 minutes. Others whispered that a merger was in the wind. By failing to state the reasoning *behind* the facts, and thus ignoring his workers' emotional need

for *context*, the president created a crisis instead of boosting morale.

The rough draft presents a potential crisis of its own. Writers typically flow along for a while, following their outlines, making their points. Then, without warning, their progress slows. The right words elude them. They lose their way—and their readers.

Even professional writers encounter thorny stretches which slow their pace. But the professionals also know the tricks of their trade—the preventive measures that avoid a full-fledged writing block. Now you can use them too:

- Worry about last things last. Clever transitions, precise punctuation and spelling, and impeccable grammar mark the work of a polished writer. But a *rough* draft is just that, a preliminary version that no one else need ever see. You need to get your ideas down on paper, the faster the better, and dotted *i*'s be damned. The niceties can come later.
- Lay aside your anxieties; either resolve them or ignore them. Get as much guidance as possible at the start. If your boss hasn't told you what he or she wants in your report, ask. If your boss can't or won't answer, forget about it. Focus on your writing, and make it as good as you can; its reception is out of your control.

- Writing requires intense concentration. When you stop writing to respond to a greeting or answer a question, it takes time and renewed effort for your brain to shift gears back to your work. A tentative idea or line of argument can be misplaced, even lost, along the way. Whenever possible, close your door and have your calls held.
- At the same time, you must transcend petty distractions. As any city room veteran can attest, moderate noise can't touch a dedicated writer on deadline. (Studies show that absolute quiet makes people *more* fidgety.)
- As you write quickly and spontaneously, new ideas and examples will pop to the surface. You didn't anticipate these revelations in your outline; perhaps you didn't even know you knew them. Welcome these intruders. They represent the most joyous and creative aspect of writing; they'll improve your work more than disrupt it. If a new idea proves *too* distracting, jot down your thought fragments and return to them later.
- Write along the path of least resistance. Neither statute nor corporate policy requires you to begin at the beginning. (The beginning, in fact, is often the *worst* place to start.) Start at the end, or skip about from section to section. As noted, you can smooth your transitions afterward.

- On long-term projects, set an artificial deadline of one week before your actual deadline. Divide your work into daily goals (pages, sections) and strive to meet them. When some inevitable slippage sets in, you'll still be ahead of the game.
- Improve your efficiency. Keep your desk neat, to avoid frustrating hunts for lost notes. Check for all necessary material and equipment. Use your most comfortable writing tools. Get your rest and exercise and avoid excessive overtime. Clear and rested heads work faster and better.
- Take short breaks to reward yourself after completing a section—but only when you're sure of what's coming next. Enjoy a cup of coffee or (better yet) a short walk, but don't sneak into a double-feature. Never stop when stuck. A rest period refreshes when you can reflect on recent success, and not worry about future failure.
- When resuming your work after a layoff, reread the last several pages. They will trigger a positive frame of mind (you wrote well then, so why not now?), and help you sustain a consistent tone and thrust.
- Don't wait for inspiration or the right mood. There is no good time or bad time to write. There is only time—and the sooner you start, the sooner you will be done.
- When you're really *hot*, when the perfect words

and ideal metaphors dance for you like circus bears, don't stop for dinner or the 6:17 to Larchmont. Don't stop for anything. These sessions are all too few and unpredictable—mysterious gifts for those wise enough to accept them.

Beating Writer's Block

As Henriette Anne Klauser notes in *Writing on Both Sides of the Brain,* writing and editing involve two distinct brain functions. We write with our right brain, the hemisphere of intuition and subjectivity. We edit with out left brain, our analytical and linear side. The problem comes when we try to do both at once—when we shackle our writing with left-brain criticism. *That's not quite right,* our left brain insists. *Can't you find a better word? Who told you that you could write, anyway? Why don't you just give up?*

And so we do, at least temporarily. We are paralyzed, pulled between two poles. We contract that dread disease called writer's block. Many doctors of literature have treated symptoms of this illness. But Klauser offers the first known cure, a process she calls "rapidwriting."

The object of rapidwriting (a.k.a. nonstop writing, free writing) is to short-circuit our left-brain critique and allow our right brain to run free. The technique is easily mastered. Simply let your words spill out without control, correction, or judgment. Write whatever comes to mind—sentence fragments, TV jingles, your own boredom or fatigue or anger. If you think the exercise is silly, write that down. If you find yourself going nowhere, write that down too. But don't stop. *Rapidwrite for at least 10 minutes at a stretch*.

According to Klauser, your best results will come after you hit a "wall" of seeming emptiness, when you think you have no more to say. At that point, your liberated right brain will spontaneously solve the problems that snagged you and allow you to resume your work. You can edit out the superfluous chatter—but do it *later*, after your writing is finished.

When writer's block crops up before a session, you must treat it as procrastination. The symptoms are classic—the "need" to sharpen one more pencil, confirm one more lunch date, double-check one more source. We procrastinate when we feel insecure or unsafe. It does no good to ignore and fight this feeling. If you force yourself to write, your prose shows it. Instead, acknowledge your fears, but without any melodrama attached. Then try to *release* those fears, as follows:

- Rapidwrite your way out. Write about procrastination and what might be holding you back. As mental health professionals know, writing is excellent therapy. A soon as you label a concern and capture it in a sentence, it seems cut down to size. Writing speeds relief faster than aspirin.
- Branch your way out with a new mid-project outline. You'll uncover new ideas, or new connections between your old ones.
- In extreme cases, get up half an hour early and start writing immediately—without a shower, caffeine, or breakfast. Scratch it out longhand in bed, if you like. In this numbed state, your right brain has the field to itself—and may surprise you with what it produces.
- Use the artificial deadline trick. When under extreme time pressure, the left brain retreats automatically to allow the right brain to meet the timetable. If you can fool yourself with an early deadline, you'll still leave time for a careful revision.

Powerful Endings

Your closing sentence (or paragraph) can be even more important than your lead. Your ending, after all, is the last thing your reader will see, and its impression will be most lasting and vivid. Hard news stories, which are cut from the bottom, commonly trail away with no harm done; newspaper readers often stop before the end of a story, anyway. But business writing is different. A bland or pointless ending is like a limp handshake at parting, a gesture that can undermine all that went before. That's especially dangerous if you want the reader to take action.

To ensure a proper ending, keep a look-out during your research. When you come across a strong anecdote or quote or conclusion, set it aside and mark it in your notes. When you outline, be sure to save it; don't waste it in the middle.

If you fail to find the ideal item, you can still close strongly with an "echo" ending. Take a word or phrase from your lead and repeat it at the end, perhaps with a twist to acknowledge the intervening material. When the echo is done correctly, readers feel the satisfaction of having come full circle.

Another worthwhile gimmick is to end your piece on a dynamic oral downbeat. Arrange your last sentence so that the last syllable is accented.

Less forceful: "That's the only way for the team as a whole to be successful."

<u>More forceful:</u>   "That's the only way for the team to suc*ceed*."

A superior ending will do more than tie ideas together. It will forge a new synthesis and make a significant final point, whether as a judgment, prediction, or recommendation. In aiming for this last bold stroke, however, beware of three pitfalls:

- Avoid closing with a cliche. ("Once again, our market share depends on our efficiency; the early bird will get the worm.") It will sound as if you ran out of steam.
- Never introduce a new topic; save that for the *next* report.
- Make sure your ending agrees with your lead.

Revision:
How Top Writers Distill Their Ideas

Professional writers know that the real action comes not during the first draft, but in the exacting process of revision. Writing is creative work. Revision is basically critical, and much closer to the stance of your readers. By the second or third time around, ideas are refined, logic is streamlined, redundancies are deleted. Weaker sentences give way to stronger, vaguer to sharper, denser to cleaner. Honest revision is not confined to correcting misplaced commas. If you can read your work with a fair eye, be prepared to make drastic changes in your architecture—even in your stated purpose.

In any case, count on spending as much time and energy on the rewrite as the original. If you do, writing will be stripped of much of its terror. You'll never need to stop stone-cold to hunt for *just* the right word; you can save the thesaurus for the second draft.

All writers develop their own methods of revision, but this seven-point plan should serve well for most:

1. Immediately after you finish writing, edit the document. Make sure that the stated purpose is what you intended. Check for logical progressions, smooth transitions, and accurate spelling and punctuation.
2. Let the document cool for two or three days. Then edit it again.
3. Set it aside one more day, then perform a third edit. Check to see if you still agree with changes made in steps 1 and 2.
4. Send the document to your typist, or word processor. When it returns, proofread and perform a final edit.
5. Have your assistant run you out a clean copy

incorporating your changes. Make any corrections, then proofread your work once again. Pay closest attention to sentences directly before and after a correction. The change may have altered your transition or flow of thought.

6. Ask an objective associate (preferably someone outside your department) to read the document and suggest improvements.

7. Consider the merit of each suggestion. Better to catch an error now, even at this late stage, than after formal distribution.

These are instances, of course, when you'll lack even one full day to edit your work. The tightest deadline, however, should allow for a meaningful revision. What you're after is a psychological distance from your work. If you don't have time to sleep on it, you can still step away from your desk and take a brisk walk around your office. When you return, you'll see the document with a fresh eye.

FORCE
AND
CLARITY

Writing is hard work because thinking is hard work. Muddled thinking can never create a lucid message, no matter how gifted the stylist. But clear thinking will produce clear writing in the hands of an able technician. This dynamic works both ways; the mental discipline of writing can make a thought still clearer, more precise.

Clarity begins with a stated purpose—an explicit expression of what you hope to achieve with your message, and what you want your reader or readers to do. Distill that purpose into a single, straight forward sentence. (If this seems difficult, you're not yet ready to write.) That sentence is your touchstone. Always keep it within reach, no matter how long your report or proposal. As Somerset Maugham once noted, "The inclination to digress is human."

Your report may be perfectly clear to any reader

who shares your expertise. *That is not good enough*. Good writing, like good driving, is defensive. Consider the least educated and sophisticated segment of your audience (whether intended or hidden). Write for that lowest common denominator—directly, without condescension. Assume nothing. Check each sentence for the slightest ambiguity; then winnow it out.

Here are some paths toward precision:

Use the Active Voice

Passive verbs kill the people in your prose. At best, they drain the energy from your writing. At worst, they make you sound evasive, unnatural, even dishonest. Business writing is traditionally passive: "Our second-quarter sales activity figures are indicating subquota performance." This smacks of corporate buck-passing, a weak-kneed reluctance to affix responsibility. (By definition, passive writing is imprecise.)

Far better to say, "We failed to meet our second-quarter sales quota." Now you are one actual person speaking to another actual person. Rapport is born.

The active voice presents verbs at their best. They show how forces (and particularly people) act upon something else—the essence of real life. When we use the who–does–what sequence, our readers can visualize the action. They can follow that action to its direct conclusion. Active verbs appeal to the senses.

> Passive voice: The stroll in the park was enjoyed by all.
>
> Active voice: We all enjoyed our stroll in the park.

Active verbs also aid the cause of brevity. The more compact your prose, the more vigorous.

> Passive voice: The reason he left the firm was that his health had failed.
>
> Active voice: Failing health forced him to leave the firm.

In some cases, a passive verb may even confuse or mislead your readers. The reason: Passivity clouds the crux of the issue—who is doing what to whom.

> Passive voice: A survey was done by the research division of the marketing department at XYZ, Inc.

Active voice:	The research division surveyed the marketing department at XYZ, Inc.

Once you recognize the problem, you can quickly make your writing more active:

- Eliminate "is," "are," "was," and "were" wherever practical.
- Inject strong verbs by deleting suffixes (*-ment, -sion, -ive, -ful,* and *-ance*) from your nouns and adjectives. It's better to acquire than to make an acquisition; to agree than to reach an agreement.

Passive voice:	He is responsible for the conversion of enemies into friends.
Active voice:	He converts enemies into friends.

- Abolish empty main clauses. Many business writers start their sentences with *it is a fact that, the reason is that,* and *it can be concluded that.* They think these constructions lend their statements authority and weight. In fact, empty clauses lend only tedium and stuffiness—not to mention extra words. By aping legalese,

they make business people sound dry, unimaginative, and inaccessible.
- Construct your sentences with common sense; begin with the logical subject. If you postpone the subject with conversational padding, your writing becomes passive and indirect.

| Passive voice: | There are three applicants with impressive resumes. |
| Active voice: | Three applicants have impressive resumes. |

The passive voice *can* be helpful in delicate situations, as when sending bad news to a superior. It is also used when the receiver is more important than the doer, or to establish an objective tone. In these cases, passive verbs move the most important element to the front of the sentence, where it belongs.

| Active voice: | A truck hit the chairman of the board. |
| Passive voice: | The chairman of the board was hit by a truck. |

Finally, choose the passive voice when you can't identify the source or performer of an action: "His heart was damaged when he was an infant."

But these are the exceptions. In most cases, business writing should be actively framed, whether in routine correspondence or a controversial report. The active voice is simply more honest—and if honesty gets you fired, you're in the wrong organization.

Use Positive Language

Your readers want to know what *is*; they'll get impatient if you keep telling them what *isn't*, even when you're describing a negative event. You skipped the meeting; your rival didn't show up. You deferred a decision; he couldn't make up his mind. Positive writing is clearer, crisper, more confident; negative language sounds tentative and noncommittal.

> Negative: He did not think the conference was worthwhile.
>
> Positive: He thought the conference was a waste of time.

In sum, use *not* only to show denial, or to contrast opposing qualities (*not* cruel, but just). If you use this little word promiscuously, you risk sounding like a George Orwell parody: "The not unblack dog chased the not unsmall rabbit across the not ungreen field." It's not hard to delete *not*; the English language holds a rich store of positives.

Negative	Positive
did not like	disliked
not honest	dishonest
not important	trivial, trifling
not central	peripheral
did not remember	forgot
not enough	insufficient
did not pay attention	ignored
not easy	difficult
did not have much confidence in	distrusted

Be Specific

Use concrete, up-close words, not vague and abstract ones. Too many reports are laden with generalizations, the boiler-plate of language. To persuade, you must demonstrate how a *particular* benefit meets the *special* needs of your reader. A tree is an oak, a sapling, or a flowering plum. It is never merely a tree. By giving the reader something to see, hear, or feel, you can make him think your thoughts.

Adjectives are most effective when they appeal to the senses (triangular, acrid, hot pink) or define precise quantities (a 37% earnings slump, a $10-per-unit discount). Vague adjectives (a living wage, a good attendance record, reasonable working conditions) are, in the words of White, "leeches that infest the pond of prose, sucking the blood of words." They pose more questions than they answer. When in doubt, readers will supply their own definitions—and they may be far different from *yours*.

Prune Dead Branches
Down to the Twigs

Every word must pull its weight—and pull in the right direction. Shirkers must be ruthlessly discarded and replaced; writers must subtract as fervently as they add. Your prose quality will soar if you evict these delinquent tenants:

- **Nouns used as verbs. Gift, host, chair, debut** and **author** are fine words in their original usage, but they sound breezy and faddish when used as verbs. In casual speech such usage is often acceptable; in formal business writing it should be avoided. You can replace such words without strain.

A poor verb:	She *debuted* as marketing director last fall.
A good noun:	She made her *debut* as marketing director last fall.

The verb forms of *input* and *interface* are bastard children of the computer age. *Impact* sounds less technical but no less silly. Disown all three.

Clumsier still are the new class of *-ize* verbs. Grown-ups set priorities; they don't prioritize.

- **Fad words** and **buzzwords**. Writing is a permanent form of communication; your report may be read, filed, and reread years later. The latest verbal vogue will not survive that long; it has no place in your prose. When business writing is filled with *parameters*, *ball-park figures*, and *game plans*, it fails *bottom-line* standards of literacy.

  The most wretched vogue of all is the ill-named *-wise* family of adverbs. "*Efficiencywise*, we came in under budget"; "*Weatherwise*, it should rain tomorrow." These prefab words tempt writers looking for shortcuts. Writing-wise, they are economical—but also vague, inept, and unacceptable. Use *-wise* only with instruction words that indicate space or direction: "Turn your watch stem *clockwise*."
- **Jargon.** Avoid technical terms, whether from

business or some other realm, unless you are writing for a technical audience. If you cannot make your point without the *Doppler effect*, be sure to define it—immediately—for your lay readers.

Business jargon is less intimidating, but no less insidious. Take *finalize*—please. When you finalize a project, are you ending it or putting it into final form? Standard language smells less of the boardroom, but it is also more precise.

- **Conditionals.** When you overuse wimp words like *would*, *can*, or *may*, you sap the verbs following them of their natural force. You also stamp yourself as an insecure writer, fearful of an unqualified statement. When you write *rather*, or *maybe*, or *perhaps*, you are *somewhat* hedging your bet. Say what you mean instead. As a rule, use *would*, *should*, *could*, and *might* only for instances of real uncertainty: "He would sign the contract if they made a concession." In other cases, the unqualified past or present tense is better.

Tentative:	If you would let me know your arrival time, I would be happy to pick you up.

| Sure: | If you let know your arrival time, I'll be happy to pick you up. |

- **Abbreviations** and **acronyms**. Words like *co.*, *ltd.*, and *UNICEF* ease the task of both writer and reader. But if readers are unfamiliar or unsure of what an abbreviation stands for, the whole business backfires. Now they must stop and try to decipher the puzzle, or else forge ahead with anxiety. To help them, spell out your terms the first time around; then place the abbreviation or acronym (a word formed from the first letters of several words) in parentheses. Thereafter you can use the short form by itself.

  Latin abbreviations (*e.g.*, *i.e.*) are both stuffy and vague. Try their modern equivalents (for example; that is) instead. When placed at the end of a list, *etc.* begs the question. If there are more items worth referring to, tell your readers what they are. If the items are insignificant, don't refer to them.

- **Cliches** are phrases that have lost their power through overuse. Once they were fresh and arresting, and so they continue to tempt us. But discriminating readers will find them wordy and irritating. Use them only if they *hit the nail* *on the head*, and you can't improve on them. These chestnuts are always expendable:

Quick as a flash
Straight from the shoulder
Last but not least
In a pinch
Abreast of the times
As plain as day
The modern business world

- **Needless intensifiers** are the pets of bureaucrats, who find haven in shades of gray: *comparatively, definitely, pretty* (as in pretty good), *quite, rather, relatively, somewhat,* and that old standby, *very.* These words are colorless, meaningless, and usually unnecessary.

  The intensifiers' wild cousins are the *absolutes,* such as *infinite, never, always, unique, perfect, totally, exact, supreme,* and *ultimate.* When used with caution, absolutes are sometimes justified—as in Supreme Being, or a perfect (baseball) game. But lazy writers lean on absolutes to make unsupported overstatements. The ruse is transparent, and the reader recoils.

  Remember that absolutes and intensifiers don't mix. An *exact* duplicate is no more than a duplicate, and is never the *most* unique.
- **Needless repetitions.** Some repetitions clarify

or lay emphasis. But after your audience gets your point, repetition becomes redundancy. A purplish, reddish-blue plum is no brighter than a purple one; the Rio Grande River is no wetter than the plain old Rio Grande.

- **Lazy adjectives.** As Voltaire once noted, "The adjective is the enemy of the noun." Two centuries haven't changed the battle lines. Writers must hold their fire, however, on *defining adjectives*, which are actually part of the nouns they precede (*math* teacher, *industrial* revolution). The bad guys are the *commenting adjectives* (or adverbs), idle gossips which waste time—those *handsome, blue-eyed, clever* saboteurs.

Some commenting words are unavoidable. But when used too often, or with too much color or enthusiasm, they tend to muddy your prose. Adjectives obscure more important words—verbs and nouns. They delay your readers from reaching your point; they tell instead of show. Like too many ruffles on a little girl's dress, they can even make that point less appealing or convincing.

To sharpen your writing, define with adjectives and describe with verbs.

<u>Adjective comment:</u>	His *voracious* eyes looked at the food in front of him.
<u>Verb description:</u>	His eyes *devoured* the food in front of him.

Beware of modern adjectives used as participles, such as *ongoing* or *offputting*. As E.B. White pointed out, no one knows exactly what these words mean. A standard participle can be changed to a verb, and its meaning will be clear: *Increasing* to *increase*, *upsetting* to *upset*, *delaying* to *delay*. But how can you *ongo* something? How can you *offput* it? You can't—so don't.

- **Pomp and affectation.** There is no such thing as "business English"—no special vocabulary, or distinctive syntax, or unique style. Good business writing, as we've noted, is simply good writing—clear, direct, concise. But some business people write as though performing a secret handshake, or some other rite known only to the initiated. They use flowery words and bloated phrases—and behave as if they're proud of them. They'll begin a letter with, "We beg to acknowledge," or promise to act "in compliance with your request."

These "zero words" clutter your writing. Far from granting an air of authority, they separate writer and reader with a pompous barrier. It serves just as well, after all, to be *with* members of a group as to be *accompanied by* them. Some other examples:

Zero words	Concise words
accord an opportunity	allow
at an early date	soon
in compliance with your request	as requested
as a matter of fact	in fact
at this point in time	at this point
at the present time	now
on the grounds that	because
notwithstanding the fact that	although
in view of the fact that	as
in view of the foregoing	given that
along the lines of	like
as to	about
for the purpose of	for
for the reason that	since
inasmuch as	since
in order to	to
in accordance with	by
in the case of	if
in the event that	if
in terms of	in
with a view to	to
with reference to	about
with regard to	about
with the result that	so that

The Thesaurus:
Your Hidden Ally

If you know what you want to say but the right word eludes you, check a thesaurus or dictionary of synonyms. Both reference works offer a wide array of words for every context, each entry with its own tone and shading. These works are invaluable writing tools, but they can be addictive—and they can be abused.

Over-ambitious writers get caught up in "elegant variation." They refuse to repeat a word within the same sentence or paragraph, or (in extreme cases) the same page. Their obsession exacts a price, however. These writers love to substitute a long or obscure word for a short and plain one, as long as variety is served. They choose *utilize* over *use*, *auspicious* for *lucky*, *spherical* for *round*, *domicile* for *home*.

What's wrong with using these elegant word alternatives? For one thing, they lie outside standard usage; as a result, they sound stilted and pretentious to your readers. For another, they teem with prefixes and suffixes, known collectively as *affixes*. They force the reader to distill the word's root (*sphere* out of *spherical*, for example), to understand what's going on. Reader comprehension is slowed; at times, it may even be blocked.

But don't throw away your thesaurus. Used with caution, it can help you become a precise and polished writer. Follow these guidelines, and no one will ever know you searched for a synonym:

- Make sure the word you choose is the right word, the *best* word, for the context. *Roget's* is not a dart board. You can't solve your puzzle by plucking words at random. If you're unsure of a synonym's meaning, look it up in a dictionary. If either of two words would seem to do, look both up to see which more closely suggests the nuances you want to convey.
- Repetition is a natural, inevitable part of writing. A repeated word can help a sentence cohere, or stress a prominent point. At worst, readers will likely ignore it; they are less sensitive about these niceties than writers.
- If a repeated noun bothers you, inject a simple pronoun for variety: *he*, *she*, *they*, or *it*. Pronouns draw less attention than nouns, and keep your prose skimming along.
- Look for synonyms at least as simple as the word you're replacing. Vary *deadly* with *lethal*, if you like, but not with *mortiferous*.

Transitions That Build
Commitment and Interest

Transitions are the ligaments of language. They connect one sentence or paragraph to the next, and steer the reader in the intended direction. Transitions show relationships between ideas: comparison, contrast, sequence, and spatial arrangement, among others. They are especially helpful in adding background or emphasis to a preceding idea: "Yesterday I was extremely busy. *In fact*, I worked until midnight."

We use connectives routinely in everyday speech. They are usually the simplest of words or phrases: *next, then, but, of course, and*. Listeners find them easy to follow.

In written English, unfortunately, many writers discard these simple constructions. Instead they resort to formal, bulky transitions—more zero words. As Rudolf Flesch and A. H. Lass note in their book *A New Guide to Better Writing*, conversational transitions will improve your writing almost every time:

Formal	Plain
likewise	and
in addition	besides, also
moreover	now, next
nevertheless	but
rather	however
that is to say	in other words
more specifically	for example
to be sure	of course
for this reason	so
hence, thus	therefore

For more subtle transitions, connect your ideas by repeating a key word, or using a pronoun to refer to a noun:

> *Junior executives* seldom see bluntness rewarded. *They* are loathe to lay their necks on any line . . . There is no good *time* or bad *time* to write. There is only *time* . . .

Smooth writers use *felt* connectives to sew seamless prose. Many sentences demand no transitions at all. They flow on like dusk into nightfall. They are connected by the logic and order of their ideas—the art that conceals art.

PUTTING STRENGTH
IN A
FEW WORDS

If brevity is the soul of wit, it is also the heart of comprehension. As William Strunk Jr. observed in his classic *The Elements of Style*:

> Vigorous writing is concise. A sentence should contain no unnecessary words, a paragraph no unnecessary sentences, for the same reason that a drawing should have no unnecessary lines and a machine no unnecessary parts.

Over-writing wastes the reader's time. It discourages quick reading and prompt response. Like teachers, lawyers, and bureaucrats, business writers load too many pages into their proposals, too many words into their sentences.

Why this glut of verbiage? For one thing, it is *tougher* to be concise than to ramble. It demands more choices and discrimination, a higher level of logic. (As Blaise Pascal, the 17th-century French philosopher, once observed: "I have made this letter longer than usual because I lack the time to make it shorter.")

Executives are trained to be concise in every other aspect of their work. They are commended and promoted for efficiency, from trimming inventory to cutting personnel expenses. Yet these same people tolerate, even glory in, verbal obesity. In this, professor Fielden notes, they are creatures of habit. Their high schools and colleges invariably rewarded them for quantity; a 15-page report, swollen to 25, would earn a better grade. When they entered their first company, they wrote as long-winded as ever, as if to get extra credit for "effort." Ironically, the people they aim to impress are more likely to flunk them. Top executives are too busy for tomes. They want brief communications with clearly stated purposes—and the two are closely linked.

Brevity is difficult, but not complicated. Weed out the redundant phrase; spare the needless detail. Above all, shorten your sentences. Short sentences give readers breathing space; too many long ones leave them gasping for air—and grasping for meaning. In a survey of college juniors and seniors, the American Press Institute found that every student understood newspaper stories with an average sentence length of eight words or less. When sentence length reached 15 words, 90 percent passed the comprehension test. But at 22 words per sentence, less than 70 percent of the students passed; at 29 words, less than half; at 40 words, less than 20 percent. When the average sentence reached an unwieldy 44 words, fewer than one of ten students could figure out what the story said.

Similar studies support the following table:

Average sentence length	Ease of understanding
8 words or less	Very easy
11 words	Easy
14 words	Fairly easy
17 words	Standard
21 words	Fairly difficult
25 words	Difficult
29 words	Very difficult

Business writers are safe if they stay at or close to the "standard" level—say, 17 to 20 words per sentence. You will also gain by setting an arbitrary maximum length. If a sentence exceeds 30 words, split it into two.

For a more precise gauge, use the *Fog Index* developed by Robert Gunning:

1. Extract a writing sample of 100 words or more. Compute the average number of words per sentence.
2. Count the words with three or more syllables. Exclude capitalized words, three-syllable

verbs ending in *es* or *ed*, and short words combined to make a longer one (e.g., *manpower*).

3. Add the figures from steps 1 and 2, and then multiply by 0.4. Round to the nearest whole number. The result is the Fog Index, which translates to years of schooling. Mass-circulation magazines rate around nine; they assume their readers have a ninth-grade education. *The Wall Street Journal* and *Fortune* score close to 12, the level of a high-school graduate. An index of 18 would require a master's degree or more.

The lower your message's index, the better— even if your audience is highly educated. Remember that people prefer reading at least one level below their capacity. Intense concentration wearies them. If forced to strain to the limit, they will grow weary and stop reading.

Like any virtue, brevity can be overdone. A writer's primary goal is to convey a purpose clearly. Brevity and clarity are first cousins, not identical twins. A quick and simple report will certainly make life easy for your readers. But if your subject is complex, those readers may lack the information to make a reasoned decision. If you make your recommendations with little supporting evidence, readers may also question the thoroughness of your research. If you lose their faith, you lose their support.

Sometimes long words are better; to explain *industrialization* without using the term might require a full paragraph. And in technical writing, particularly, the simplest word is often less accurate than some polysyllabic mouthful. Use your judgment, and decide what counts—exact meaning, or ease of understanding.

Remember that you are guiding most readers along unfamiliar trails; your mission is to keep them out of the underbrush, and bring them safely home. A grizzled city editor said it best to a rookie reporter, when asked the appropriate length for a school board story: "Write what it's worth."

GRAMMAR AND SYNTAX: TIPS FROM THE PROS

A full discussion of grammar is beyond the scope of this Report. Your best tools are an unabridged dictionary for spelling and usage, a thesaurus for the right word in the right place, and a general guide to punctuation and structure. (*The Elements of Style*, by Strunk and White, is venerable but not dated).

As educated people, most business writers have an instinctive grasp for grammar and syntax (word order). Still, it pays to be vigilant over troublesome areas. For example:

Parallel Construction

The vice president was responsible for *budgeting* the ad campaign and *approving* a new slogan. To be parallel, each phrase or direct object must begin with the same part of speech. Without parallelism, both logic and felicity suffer.

<table>
<tr><td>Not parallel:</td><td>The new health club will have room for both a pool and playing tennis.</td></tr>
<tr><td>Parallel:</td><td>The new health club will have room for both a pool and tennis courts.</td></tr>
<tr><td>Also parallel:</td><td>The new health club will have room for both swimming and tennis.</td></tr>
</table>

In business writing, parallel items may be set off with bullets.

Our new ad campaign will:

- boost company morale;
- rejuvenate our image;
- expand our market share.

Parallel constructions are clearer when you repeat prepositions, articles (*the, a*) or pronouns before each element. Repetitions may seem heavy-handed, but they prevent confusion.

| Less clear: | The secretary was tired of her duties, boss, and pay scale. |
| More clear: | The secretary was tired of her duties, her boss, and her pay scale. |

Parellism is muddled when conjunctions (*either, neither, both, also*) come too early in the sentence, rather than just before parallel objects.

| Confusing: | The chairman was neither loyal to the board nor to the shareholders. |
| Clear: | The chairman was loyal neither to the board nor to the shareholders. |

Proper Pronouns

When pronouns are used for nouns, they must agree in number. For example: "All *writers* must tell *their* stories."

Depending on how a pronoun performs, it is either in the *subjective* case (I, he, she, we, they) or the *objective* case (me, him, her, us, them). *You* does double duty: "*You* threw the ball to me, and I threw it back to *you*."

When a pronoun modifies the noun, deleting the noun will point you toward the right case: "*We* (managers) joined the profit-sharing plan."

When a pronoun follows *as* or *than*, mentally add the omitted words. The proper case will be obvious: "Her son was taller than *she* (was tall)."

Dangling Modifiers

To avoid ambiguity or distortion, keep descriptive or qualifying phrases close to the words they modify. Mistakes can be unintentionally comical.

Surreal:	I shot the bear in my bathrobe.
Real;	I shot the bear while wearing my bathrobe.
Also real:	Wearing my bathrobe, I shot the bear.

Dangling modifiers crop up most often at the start of a sentence. Errant writers begin with an introductory clause and then fail to sort out their subjects.

Dangling:	While passing her desk, the lights flickered.
Correct:	While *he* passed her desk, the lights flickered.

But modifiers also dangle at the ends of sentences, often as casualties of the passive voice. As before, you can solve the problem by adding a noun or pronoun:

Dangling:	The report was easy after finishing the outline.
Correct:	The report was easy after we finished the outline.

The same cure works for *elliptical clauses*—dependent clauses that dangle because they fail to share the main clause's subject:

Dangling:	When still a pup, the veterinarian wouldn't charge me.
Correct:	When *my collie* was still a pup, the veterinarian wouldn't charge me.

Punctuation

Punctuation marks support structure, logic, and meaning. More than any other device they make our writing easier to follow. As Flesch and Lass point out, punctuation reflects the pauses and stresses of everyday speech:

	Between words	Between Sentences
Normal pause	White space	Period
Shorter pause	Hyphen	Semicolon or colon
Longer pause	Dash	Paragraph

Normal stress	Normal type or writing
Unstressed	Parentheses or two dashes
Stressed	Italics or underlining

Of all the marks, semicolons are most underused and underrated. They allow writers to show a clear link between two thoughts while simplifying sentence structure.

Complex:	Construct your sentences with common sense by beginning with the logical subject.
Simple:	Construct your sentences with common sense; begin with the logical subject.

The English language is a living vehicle for ideas, not a rigid set of dogma. There are times when grammatical rules are made to be broken. There are times when it is appropriate to split an infinitive ("It's hard to really understand him"), or to end with a preposition ("He was the best candidate I could think of"), or to begin a sentence with *and* or *but*. Or even to write an incomplete sentence.

English is for the ear, as well as the eye; if an unorthodoxy sounds correct when you say it aloud, it likely *is* correct. But before you break the rules, make sure that you know them. Then break them selectively. An occasional liberty becomes a gimmick if it is overused.

STYLE
AND
TONE

Style is simply defined as the way in which a message is expressed, as distinguished from its substance. As such, it is only a means to your end. Your first intent is to gain action from your readers by conveying your objective. Style can help by gaining your readers' attention and sympathy, even if they've never met you. You are no longer strangers because they hear and like your tone of voice.

The traditional style for business writing is stiff and formal to a fault. Executives are cool and impersonal where they should be friendly and conversational. They treat words like Cuban cigars—the bigger the better. They shun finesse whenever raw power will do.

And so their style defeats them, no matter how good their ideas. A letter which begins, "It has come to our attention that . . ." has all the warmth of a dunning for payment past due. Rather than draw reader and writer together, this kind of writing widens the gap. An offensive style can block a sale, lose a customer, blow a promotion, or even cost you a job.

When you adopt a style or tone, you adopt a role—and you confer one on your readers. To make your readers relax, write with *the least formality* your relationship or context allows. If you are the "boss," all unsmiling authority, they are the underlings. If you are the pompous know-it-all, they are the ignorant children. If you are a stilted robot, graceless and mechanical, they become robots too.

Great literary style is a high art given to few. Good business style is less mysterious. If you follow the principles of clarity, brevity, and grammar, your writing will become direct and confident—the backbone of style. You need not agonize over fine shadings of tones. With time and practice, your personality will surface, spontaneously. The reader will absorb your spirit, your habits, your biases. Your writing will sound as you do when talking at your best.

That direct baseline style is not quite as artless as it appears, however. To develop it, you must tune your ear to the connotations of words as well as to their meanings. A positive style requires positive words, especially when dealing with problems, money, or personalities. For example:

Positive	Negative
frugal	stingy
methodical	fanatical
firm	rigid
colorful	garish
problem	disaster
setback	fiasco, debacle
expensive	exorbitant
generous	extravagant
uninformed	ignorant
youthful	immature
mature	aging

Ideally, a business writer should seek to project a forceful, friendly tone. But your stylistic *strategy* will vary with each writing situation. It will reflect your power relative to the reader's, and how you want the reader to react. Consider how differently you speak to superiors or subordinates, to peers or clients, to a person you are promoting or one you are firing. Effective writing addresses these distinctions through style. Consider five style categories, offered by Professor Fielden:

1. The Forceful Style

Here the writer has the power to make an action request, or to say no to a subordinate. This style cuts off any hope of further negotiation. It is appropriate for boss to subordinate communications. It may also be appropriate for the cover letter to a more passive, impersonal report. To adapt this style:

- **Use the active voice.** Your sentences are your couriers; they should be giving orders, not taking them. By telling someone, "Correct this error immediately," you are assuming both authority and responsibility.
- **Stand up and be counted by using personal pronouns,** even in uncomfortable situations. Write: "I have decided against funding your project," rather than "Unfortunately, funds for your project will not be forthcoming." You're an executive, not a politician.
- **Write most sentences in subject-verb-object order.** Don't dilute your message with some weak-kneed dependent clause. ("After much consideration and careful weighing of the pros

and cons, I have decided . . .") It's your decision; don't apologize for it.

- **Make your point in the sentence's main clause.** Write: "We selected your proposal, although competition was fierce," and not "Although we selected your proposal, competition was fierce."
- **Expunge all wimp words and vague third-person pronouns.** The following sort of sentence will undermine your power: "Some might conclude we were somewhat hasty in canceling our contract with you."

2. The Passive Style

This style suits the bringing of bad news, particularly when the messenger is writing "up" to a superior or client. It does not produce "good" writing; you are shrouding responsibility and softening your point. It is a defensive, elusive style, one more appropriate for a professional diplomat. There are times, however, when the most you can hope for is to be spared the reader's wrath. For this style:

- **Use the passive voice.** At the least, it will push the sentence subject to the end of the sentence, implicitly relieving you of responsibility. With clever handling, it can bury the subject entirely: "The cost analysis was completed several weeks after it had been projected." (In other words, it missed the deadline.)

- **Never give imperative orders.** Write: "A prompter review of our preliminary findings would help the team conform to its timetable," and not "Respect our time and give us faster feedback."

- **Use wimp words.** And if you do proceed, *perhaps*, in a round-about way, you *may possibly* mollify your reader.

- **Attribute negative statements to faceless, impersonal "others."** Write: "It is possible that some observers might be unconvinced by your proposal," and not "I cannot agree with your proposal."

- **Use longer words, longer sentences, denser paragraphs.** Granted, this runs counter to all general wisdom on writing. But in delicate, negative situations, your *purpose* is to soften the blow. Abruptness can be deadly. If your readers feel slapped, they'll be tempted to slap back. But heavy language, like milk before alcohol, will slow the impact of your news.

3. The Personal Style

This is writing at its most relaxed and conversational. It usually fits good-news situations, action requests to associates or customers, or informal social contexts. When done well, personal writing bears the stamp of both writer and specific reader. It could never be mistaken for a form letter.

- **Use contractions.** Don't believe your high-school English teacher; they're perfectly acceptable. Without them, you will sound stuffy.
- **Use personal pronouns, particularly "you" and "I."** Gossip appeals to us because it considers our prime interest in life: other people. The logical subject of a sentence is *always* a person. The most technical scientific research can be converted into an indoor adventure story, the struggle of a human mind to find a new order of things.

  By using personal pronouns, you stress the humanity of your subject—and your desire to get through to another live person who will read your words. When giving good news, be a part of it. When answering a complaint, be genuinely sympathetic. If you're writing for a group (such as stockholders) and want to stress your shared interest, use "we" whenever you can.

Impersonal: Your presentation was warmly received.

Personal: I heartily enjoyed your presentation.

Impersonal: The merger would assure dominance in this market.

Personal: The merger would assure us the market edge we need.

"Human-interest" nouns will also enliven your writing, whether used as subjects or objects. The more *aunts*, and *infants*, and *companions* in your prose, the more accessible it will be.

- **When referring to others, use names rather than titles.** For informal messages, first names are best.
- **Summon everyday images.** Speak to your readers as if sitting down with them for a cup of coffee.
- **Use short sentences.** Capture the rhythm of normal speech: "I discussed your report with Helen. She liked it, and so did I."
- **Interject personal anecdotes and opinions.** You are *involved*, not neutral and removed. Positive feelings need not be hidden. An exam-

ple drawn from your own experience will both clarify your point and warm your style.

- **Insert colloquialisms and idioms.** These down-home terms will *perk up* your prose, or bring a dry, complex topic *down to earth*. They shoot formality *dead in its tracks*. Use them only if they feel natural, however. There is nothing stuffier than a stiff idiom. *"By the same token,"* resist any urge to place your phrase within quotation marks.
- **Introduce yourself—and then get out of the way.** Business writing deals with objective reality—a problem, a proposal, an observation. These subjects are central, not their messenger. Besides, only egomaniacs assume that their every thought and whimsy will be of interest to others.

Remember that you aim to persuade your readers, not to impress them. Your cleverness and warmth are positive qualities, to be sure—but only if they help you make your point.

4. The Impersonal Style

In a formal market or feasibility study, your mission is to gather and analyze the facts, as objectively as possible. In these situations, too much personality will make you *less* persuasive. It will distract the reader and detract from your research. An impersonal approach is also standard for technical and scientific writing, and can help you through negative situations.

- **Avoid personal pronouns.** The exception is the corporate "we," which is faceless and quite impersonal. Write: "We wonder if the plant will survive," and not "I doubt the plant will survive."
- **Refer to people by their titles.** It is their job descriptions that matter, not their names.
- **Disappear when desirable through the passive voice.** Write: "Funding for the laboratory was suspended," and not "I suspended funding for the laboratory."
- **Use complex sentences and long paragraphs.** They will add weight and gravity to your findings.
- **Avoid contractions.** They project an offhand tone which runs counter to your purpose.

5. The Colorful Style

Liveliest of all, this style can make good news sound even more enthusiastic. It is highly persuasive, and is commonly found in advertisements and sales letters.

- **Be generous with adjectives and adverbs.** Write: "This *hard-hitting* proposal will *surely* save our *dwindling* corporate resources," and not "This proposal will save our corporate resources."

  Don't get carried away, however. Too many adjectives will make you sound as though you're selling vacuum cleaners.

- **Pepper your language with simile** (A is like B) and **metaphor.** (A "is" B). Both figures of speech are comparisons between things that are in general unlike.

  A simile is an express comparison. It uses such words as *like* and *as* to make the comparison. A metaphor is an implied comparison. It is made without the use of comparative words as connectors.

Similes:	The office is like a giant bee-hive; busy, highly productive, and filled with swarms of specialized workers. You can use this report as your Baedeker.
Metaphors:	We march to a different drummer. The board's trouble is that it is a turtle. Whenever it sees the shadow of something unpleasant, it quickly withdraws into its shell and stays there until it's certain the danger is past.

- **As direct questions.** Engage your reader with simulated conversation: "Aren't you fed up with investments that never pay off?"
- **Resist exaggerations and sweeping generalizations.** These pitfalls are endemic to colorful writing, but they also lurk within other styles. A single overstatement can destroy a reader's faith in a writer's judgment. Is your product really *the best* that ever rolled off an assembly line, or merely *one of the best*? Are bankers *always* conservative, or *typically* so. A bit of modesty in your assertions will pay dividends in reader confidence.

Your chosen style helps your readers form an image of you, the writer. By "hearing" your voice, they construct a personal relationship which makes them more receptive to your ideas. You must therefore be careful to maintain the same style throughout your message, with no lapses. If you waver, your readers will feel confused and alienated. If you hold firm and steady, you will win their trust.

Avoiding Sexism

Written English is a sexist language. Business writing, after generations of male dominance in the boardroom, is even more so. The "chairman of the board" will not easily be replaced by a "chairwoman" or "chairperson." Still, modern executives should strive to remove sexism from their messages. Ignoring the issue risks needless offense to a growing portion of their audience. In some situations (performance appraisals, notices of job openings), a thoughtless pronoun can be grounds for a lawsuit.

To avoid sexist writing, observes communication consultant Judy E. Pickens, you must replace "limiting or insensitive habits with positive alternatives." For example:

- **Expand male-oriented terms to include both sexes.** If *chairperson* seems awkward (and it is), substitute *presiding officer, chair,* or *moderator*. Use *executive* instead of *businessman; staff hours* instead of *man-hours; supervisor* instead of *foreman*. Other sexist terms are more insidious:

Sexist	Non-Sexist
man-made	synthetic
manpower	workforce
gentlemen's agreement	informal agreement
you and your wife	you and your spouse

- **Avoid the masculine pronoun "he" when referring to both sexes.** There are several ways around this knotty problem:

1. Use the third-person *plural* form. Write: "Employees are evaluated on *their* anniversary dates," and not "Each employee is evaluated on *his* anniversary date."
2. Eliminate the pronoun: "Performance is evaluated on the employee's anniversary date."
3. Substitute *you* or *one*: "You are evaluated on your anniversary date."

Any of these options is preferable to "Each employee's work is evaluated on *his or her* anniversary date." Such "dueling pronouns" sound self-conscious and awkward.

- **Neuter your nameless salutations.** Depending on the message's formality, write: "To Whom It May Concern," or "Greetings," and not "Dear Sir." When extending a more personal invitation to a couple, treat both people equally.

Sexist	Non-sexist
Mr. and Mrs. John Hicks	John and Carol Hicks
Mr. Jones and Jo Smith	Jay Jones and Jo Smith
Alex and Miss Jackson	Alex and Marjorie

- **Be wary of Ms.** Salutations to women of unknown marital status are trickiest. While Ms. may be technically acceptable, some women are offended by it. To be safe, telephone the woman and ask what she prefers. If the salutation is important enough to worry you, it's important enough for a phone call.
- **Be reasonable.** Some terms define gender without a shred of sexism. *Host* and *hostess* are always acceptable; *actor* and *actress* (or *leading man* and *leading lady* are indispensable.
- **Watch for racism too.** Racism is a less common problem for educated writers. Still it pays to steer clear of stereotyping adjectives, even in jest (*wild* Irishmen, *frugal* Jews, *inscrutable* Chinese). Refer to *blacks* rather than *Blacks*— unless you plan to use *Whites*.

BRINGING
POWER TO
WHAT YOU WRITE

To this point, *Power Business Writing* has addressed general procedures and principles of written communication. Armed with these guidelines, we now turn to specific applications.

Reports

Reports are the basic instruments of business writing. If an event or situation has any long-term significance, it must be recorded for future reference. *Feasibility reports* gauge a new project's odds of success. *Investigative reports* analyze topics and offer the writer's recommendations. *Progress reports* keep executives up to date on a project's status, schedule, and expenses. *Trip reports* review business trips for the benefit of those who could not go. *Trouble reports* help management pinpoint the source of a problem and make necessary changes.

Structure your reports to serve your purpose—the action step you hope to accomplish. You have three basic options:

- **Straight-line structures** are simplest, and are best-suited for pure information (without conclusions) or how-to-do-it reports. They're easy to organize, but can be dull if too mechanical.
- **Building-block structures** use a brief introduction, then layer one observation or finding onto the next. They build your logic bit by bit, from observations to conclusions to recommendations. This structure is most persuasive for developing a complex argument, but it also holds back primary material—your punchline—till the end. Without rigid self-discipline, writers may get distracted by a point of more interest to them than to their audience. Business readers are on company time; they are too busy for mystery stories.
- **Inverted pyramid structures** are borrowed from journalism. Here you place the most important items (including your summary) at the top, and the less important items toward the bottom. Most executives prefer to receive inverted pyramid reports; they find them clear and direct. There is a drawback: conclusions are

presented before supporting evidence. Readers must credit a writer with good faith, or at least suspend their disbelief until they reach the body of the report.

In school, most students are trained in the building-block technique. Many business writers find it difficult to break that old pattern. Rather than struggle, they can continue to use building blocks while they write, then rearrange their reports to flip their conclusions to the top—an easy task with any word-processing program.

Regardless of type, most formal reports are expected to include the following components, in order of presentation:

- A **preface** (written by the author), a **foreword** (written by someone else), or both. They offer background on the subject or why the report was written. If appropriate, a preface also includes acknowledgments to thank others who assisted in the work. Keep in mind, however, that some readers routinely skip prefaces and forewords, confident that they will miss no essentials. Write your preface in the same spirit; if you include any critical material, be prepared to repeat it in the body of your text.
- **Abstracts** (also known as descriptive or indicative abstracts) are the narrative equivalent of a table of contents. Rarely longer than several

sentences, they describe your purpose, scope, and methods, but only in general terms. They are most appropriate for informational surveys and progress reports.

- **Summaries** (also known as informative abstracts) supply a more specific digest of what is to come, and may run as long as two pages. Like a preface, however, a summary must stand on its own; it cannot refer to any tables, illustrations, or bibliographies elsewhere in the report. All unfamiliar symbols, abbreviations, and acronyms must be spelled out.

- **Executive summaries** are designed for top managers who must decide policy, funding, or personnel questions based on the report. Since an executive summary may be the *only* part of the report read by these rushed decision-makers, it must include your purpose, scope, and findings, all in brief but adequate detail. It must highlight your recommendations, the executive's prime concern.

  For maximum impact, condense your executive summary into a single page, even if you must single-space to do so. At most, write no more than 10 percent of your report's total length. At the same time, however, avoid grammatical shortcuts; connect your points with transitions like *however*, *for example*, and *in conclusion*. If your executive summary reads like an instruction manual, it will sound brusque and unappealing.

- **Contents lists** should include a table of contents as well as a list of tables and illustrations, when applicable. Be generous with headings and subheadings in your table of contents. The more detailed the list, the easier it will be for your readers to find what they're looking for.
- **Introductions** are among the leading causes of writer's block—especially when writers attempt to do them sequentially, before the body of their reports. The problem is obvious. An introduction must consider your subject, purpose, scope, and point of view, in addition to your plan for developing these points. As veteran writers know, however, your point of view tends to evolve as you write, even when you start with a very detailed outline. The solution is simple: Write your introduction at the end of your report, then insert it in the proper place. Or draft an introductory sketch at the beginning, add additional ideas as you proceed, and rewrite a more formal version at the end.
- The **body** of your report discusses procedures, methodology, and observations—*how* you came to know what you know. Here, finally, space is no longer at a premium; include all the detail you believe is pertinent.
- The **conclusion** is a report's focal point, the target at which you've been aiming all along. It

tells what you learned (but not *how* you learned it, which comes in the body), and leads logically to your **recommendations.** Conclude as decisively as your evidence warrants, but no more so. (In cases of conflicting or insufficient evidence, the honest course may be to *omit* any conclusions. If you do so, use this section to explain why.) You have journeyed full circle; your conclusions should satisfy your introduction's promise, and refrain from injecting new issues or concerns.

- **Appendixes** range from notes, charts, and tables to raw computer printouts, statistical calculations, and case histories—any supplementary material that is too unwieldy for the body of the report.
- **Glossaries** define special or technical terms which may be unfamiliar to your readers. They work best when their definitions are brief and straightforward, and when they assume no technical background.

Proposals

A proposal is a sales presentation, whether to win a government contract or to gain approval for a project within your own company. If written effectively, a proposal will convince the decision-maker (in this case, the buyer or senior management) that you can deliver on your promise of goods or services—and on the "buyer's" terms.

In a *solicited proposal,* you are responding to a customer's formal call for help, often called a *request for proposal* (RFP). Here you must show that you can beat the competition. But your task is not as simple as it sounds; about one of every two proposals is rejected because it failed to understand the customer's stated problem. If you have any questions about the RFP, ask them before you write your proposal. As a side benefit, you may gain insight into the buyer's quirks or biases. *Never assume what a customer needs.*

In an *unsolicited proposal,* you must first show that a need exists; you must shape and (in extreme cases) even create that need. Only then can you prove that your company or department is best-qualified.

Like reports, proposals follow a conventional ordering:

- An **abstract** or **summary** or both, followed by a **contents list.** All three perform the same functions as in a report.
- An **introduction** restates the problem you're planning to solve, acknowledges any likely difficulties, then concisely states your conclusion. It emphasizes customer benefits (usually savings or profits) and predicts your success rate.

- A **technical plan** (or **work statement**) describes specific tasks, in the order you plan to complete them. It also explains why you have chosen a given route over available alternatives.
- A **management plan** shows how you will administer the contract. It identifies your personnel on an organization chart, and also outlines your timetable, reporting procedures, quality control measures, accounting practices, labor relations, and company background.
- A **capabilities and experience** section expands upon the qualifications of key managers assigned to the project, and includes their resumes. It also promotes your company or department with pertinent data from annual reports, past proposals, press releases, and newspaper and magazine clippings.
- A **cost analysis** lists all expenses, from work hours to facilities, utilities, and material. At the RFP's request, it may be placed in a separate volume.
- Frame your **conclusion** in a spirit of cooperation: "I'm sure we can get together to address your needs."

Why do proposals fail? Sometimes failure is unavoidable; a rival enjoys a competitive advantage (or favored status with the buyer) that you cannot overcome. At other times, as noted above, the RFP is misconstrued. But there are other, more subtle sources of failure that a knowing writer can overcome:

- **A dry, stiff, or tentative tone.** The best salespeople are warm, conversational, and confident. Your proposals should emulate them. Write about what you *will* do, not what you *could* or *would* do.
- **An emotional or extravagant appeal.** Written proposals are *soft* sells; you're not hawking a dinette set, after all. Treat your customers as peers and professionals. Be honest and concrete. Watch out for excessive underlining or use of bold-face type; you'll project yourself as shrill and pushy. Convince your reader the way *you* would wish to be convinced—with hard facts, clear numbers, and compelling logic.
- **A disorangized presentation.** List your strongest points first, where they can't be ignored. To lend your proposal a positive urgency, highlight your main action steps and dates. Place your project manager's name and phone number on both the cover and title page, in case the customer needs to reach you in a hurry.

Memoranda

Memos are used for everyday internal company communications which don't require a longer or more formal report. They announce policies, assign responsibilities, report on progress, transmit documents, confirm conversations (and commitments), and instruct workers. Well-written memos prevent misunderstandings and boost company spirit and unity. Unlike oral discussions, they offer an objective record which transcends any one person's memory. A memo may be in error—but at least all concerned can refer to the record and agree what the error *is*.

To do their job, memos need to be clear and accurate. A jot outline will ensure that you touch on all important points. Stylistic concerns take a back seat; brevity is more important than in other forms, and the writer has less latitude in organization. The standard memo opening, for example, is brisk and direct:

To:
From:
Date:
Subject:

After filling in the blanks, it's time to take the plunge: State your purpose in the first paragraph, and preferably in the first sentence. If all or some of your readers are unfamiliar with your subject, you might also include some brief background information. But don't delay your main idea; work the background in around it. For example:

All new employees *must* complete and sign their federal work authorization forms within three days of their hiring. As you know, Congress passed the Immigration Reform and Control Act in an effort to stem the flow of illegal aliens into the U.S. workforce. . . .

Your lead should be simple and specific. Whenever possible, it should emphasize measurable benefits or costs (in dollars) or deadlines (with dates). Less tangible concerns, such as work environment or company morale, can be mentioned further down.

There are only two exceptions to this straight-from-the-shoulder approach: 1) when you know your readers are skeptical about your claim or contention; 2) when you're disagreeing with your boss or other superiors. In the first case, simply list your points, from most to least specific. In the second, practice the "slow-no" technique, which we'll treat in detail in our discussion of business letters.

An *issue memo* is lengthier and more complex,

closer in spirit to a report's executive summary. While its focus is narrow, it must include sufficient information to lead a manager to a well-informed decision. When writing an issue memo, be sure to:

- Define the issue, either in a declarative sentence or as a question.
- Offer your recommendations to solve the problem or take advantage of the opportunity.
- Discuss the policy (briefly) along with alternatives and controversies, if any.
- Consider the fiscal impact, with a thorough analysis of potential savings or costs. Show where the money will come from to cover any new expenses.
- Outline one or more action steps to implement the policy. (Check company practice before including action steps; some executives will feel undue pressure to approve the policy in question, and resent it.)

Letters

While memos are meant for inhouse distribution, letters go primarily outside the company. As a result, you must follow more conventions when writing them. Not so long ago, business letters were universally stiff, impersonal, and written in the passive voice. It was *this company* and never *we; the undersigned,* rather than *I.*

But in modern business writing, a letter's style follows its function—a direct attempt, from one person to another, to communicate and persuade. Today you write to your addressee as if you had met the individual in person and were talking across your desk. A personal touch gets the reader on your side, no matter how technical or formal your subject. To inject that touch, you can:

- **Use personal pronouns,** especially *I* and *you.*
- **Use contractions** liberally.
- **Be gracious.** Write *please* and *thank you* when requesting favors. Words like *appreciate* and *grateful* won't hurt your cause, either.
- **Use an informal complimentary close,** such as *cordially* (least formal), *truly,* or *sincerely.* If you're making a polite request, try *yours truly* or *yours sincerely.*

Letters follow a strict format. If you use letterhead stationery (which includes your "inside" address), you always begin by noting the date, normally flushed at the right margin. From there you move to the salutation, your first sticky spot. Never have two or three words caused more confusion and uncertainty. You'll avoid a gaffe, however, if you follow these guidelines.

- If you're on a first-name basis with the addressee, use a comma (*Dear John,*). If not, use a colon (*Dear Mr. Johnson:*).
- If you're writing more or less blind, a formal approach (*Dear Sir* or *Dear Madam*) is least likely to offend anyone.
- If you're unsure of a woman's preferred title (*Ms., Miss,* or *Mrs.*), call her secretary to find out.

Like other brief communications, letters afford no time to ramble. You should usually state your point in your lead sentence. By the second sentence, restate both the date *and* subject of the reader's last letter to you. Aside from clarifying the matter, this will preserve legal continuity in the exchange.

The exception, once again, is when you present bad news. Because the letter is more personal and direct than other forms, the "slow no" technique is even more exacting. While you don't want to raise false hopes, strive always to cushion your blow, whether you're rejecting a job applicant or cutting off funds to an unsuccessful project:

- **Acknowledge the facts of the matter.** In the process, acknowledge your reader's problems and try to say something positive (*and* truthful) about him or her.
- **Build your argument carefully,** fact by fact.
- **Cite available support material for your con-**

clusion. Don't argue with the reader; just stick to your facts.

- **Say no, politely but firmly.** Don't suggest that you are open to persuasion or that the decision might be reversed—unless that is indeed the case.
- **Close quickly.** But first use your imagination; if you can think of an alternative that might help the reader, suggest it.

Throughout a slow-no letter, use positive (or at least neutral) language to soften the message as much as possible. A passive style is recommended.

Negative: Since you failed to meet our experience requirements, you can't get a job here.

Neutral: As our experience requirements were not met, a position cannot be offered at this time.

Negative: Because of a seasonal market slump, we must lay off 12 of the division's 20 workers.

Positive: Despite a seasonal market slump, we can retain eight of the division's 20 workers.

Technical Writing

Before writing a technical report, decide which concepts can be explained to a lay-person and which are *too* complex. (The second category can be confined to your appendixes, for the benefit of other experts.) That settled, make your technical writing just as personal and vigorous as any other communication. Picture your lay audience as if you were speaking to foreigners—people who are just as smart as you, but who grew up with another language. When in doubt, *explain;* assumptions can be hazardous.

To combine scientific objectivity with a readable, personal style, you'll want to:

- **Use the active voice and write in the first person**—but with modesty.
- **Define technical terms** by comparing them to things familiar to your readers. Take time to develop colorful analogies and metaphors.
- **Describe your material in sensory terms;** tell how things look, sound, and feel. Aside from educating the reader and adding a literary tone to your work, descriptions lend credibility to scientific writing.
- **Include numbers only where they're critical.** Too many of them will discourage lay readers.

- **When the precise technical term is important, don't be afraid to use it**—as long as you promptly define it the first time.
- **Place your glossary *in front* of your introduction,** rather than at the end of your report. It will be more useful to your readers, and less likely to be missed.

Resumes

A resume is a type of proposal—a job proposal where you are selling yourself. To be effective, your resume must leap at a personnel director's eye. If it is run-of-the-mill and mass-produced, you will be lost among scores of other unimaginative applicants.

In most cases, you'll do better by "teasing" with a one-page letter of application, which promises a resume at the employer's request. That single sheet will stand apart from the two- and three-page bundles around it.

When composing the resume itself, shape it both to your background and the needs of the employer. The normal format leads with your *employment objective*, followed by *experience* and *education*. But if you are a recent college graduate with special skills and few job credentials, describe your education *before* your experience. If you've been at one company most of your working life, but with varying responsibilities, you might organize your experience section by *function* rather than by employer. (The function format also helps to veil gaps caused by unemployment.)

Some other sales tips:

- In stating your employment objective, stress how you can help the company, rather than how you plan to use the company to further your career.
- Use power verbs to describe your achievements: *created, administered, planned, developed, led, organized.* Avoid *helped, assisted, tried, attempted.*
- Include eye-catching numbers to quantify your achievements.
- Specify promotions and pay increases, but *not* your present salary. If the company offers you a job, you should be paid according to your value and experience, not what your last employer happened to pay you.
- Federal law prohibits employers from demanding personal information, such as age or marital status. If you think such data might *help* your cause, however, feel free to volunteer it. A married man of 25, for example, is widely deemed more mature than a single man of the same age.
- Make yourself available; include home and work phone numbers on the front page.

PAGE FORMATS
THAT GET
IDEAS ACROSS

A business document does not persuade by clarity or style alone. Its physical appearance can either invite further scrutiny or discourage the most interested readers. For example:

- **White space** makes your facts more accessible and each page more inviting. Readers are deterred less by a thick report than by densely packed pages. To charm your audience, use short paragraphs, frequent headings, and ample margins (one-and-one-quarter inches at the top and sides, and one-and-one-half inches at the bottom).
- **Lists** of parallel items are most easily read when set off with bullets, asterisks, or numbers. Aside from furnishing white space, the bullet format ensures that no item will be overlooked.

- **Footnotes** make a page grayer, especially when printed in smaller type than the body of the text. Depending on your company's custom, you can improve the appearance of your message by consolidating your notes at the back of the document.

COMMON
WORD BLUNDERS
YOU *MUST* AVOID

Writing is a series of fine decisions. Some can be decided by broad rules. Others are strictly judgment calls, best left to the spontaneity of the process. But many decisions lie in the ticklish realm of word choice and usage. There is no great rule of thumb which can ease this task. To master the realm, you must learn correct usages at the start, then practice them in your writing. In this closing glossary, we'll discuss some of the knottier problems you'll face.

Please remember, however, that good writing is more than correctness. To write is not to march in step, but to sculpt ideas, visualize images, harness words, and discover new connections. Writers need to respect conventions and revere accuracy, to be sure. But most of all they need lively minds.

With that in mind, go over the following words to be sure that you are using each one correctly.

affect/effect

Similar pronunciation helps muddle their meanings. As a verb, *affect* means to influence, while *effect* means to cause or bring about.

- The workers' petition *affected* management's decision on flex-time.
- The vice president *effected* a new flex-time policy.

As a noun, *effect* means a result or outcome. The noun *affect* is a psychological term for feeling or emotion. It rarely appears in general usage.

aggravate/irritate

Aggravate means to make something worse. It is **not** a synonym for *irritate*, which means to bother or annoy.

The cigarettes *irritated* his lungs and *aggravated* his emphysema, until he had to quit his job.

altogether/all together

Altogether means wholly, completely, or thoroughly. But a group is *all together* if its members are in the same place at the same time.

allusion/delusion/illusion

Allusion is an indirect reference; *delusion* a false belief; *illusion* a deceptive image.

- The candidate made a veiled *allusion* to his opponent's shady background.
- The voters harbored the *delusion* that both rivals were honest men.
- The incumbent's ad campaign bolstered the *illusion* that he ran a clean administration.

among/between

In most cases, *between* expresses a relationship involving two people or things (*between* you and me), while *among* is used with groups of three or more (you are *among* friends). Writers stumble most often when relating two items at a time within a larger group.

Three recent elections were *between* Kennedy and Nixon, Carter and Ford, and Reagan and Mondale.

as/like

Here lies one of the most troublesome choices in modern English—a famous controversy ever since Winston tasted good "like a cigarette should." The grammarians howled (correctly) that *like* was only a poor preposition, and so could not introduce a clause (a group of words with both a subject and complete predicate—in this case *cigarette* and *should*, respectively). Clauses must be introduced by conjunctions—by words like *as*.

- He plays *like* a prodigy.
- He plays *as* the great Schnabel once played.

In spoken English, the distinction is often blurred and no one seems to care very much. In written English, the convention still demands respect.

assure/ensure/insure
These three are close in meaning as well as sound, and even dictionaries disagree about their proper places. You'll be safe, however, if you limit "assure" to "making a person sure of something." To *ensure* is to make sure in a more general sense; to *insure* provides for payments in the event of loss.

- He *assured* me he would make good on the loan.
- The Federal Reserve Board *ensured* there would be no inflation.
- We *insured* the house against theft, fire, and liability suits.

because/since
For maximum clarity, use only *because* to show a causal relationship between two events. *Since* works most clearly to express a relationship in time.

<u>Ambiguous:</u>	*Since* his mother came to visit, he has skipped his weekly poker game.
<u>Clear:</u>	*Because* his mother came to visit, he has skipped his weekly poker game.
<u>Also clear:</u>	Ever *since* his mother came to visit, he has skipped his weekly poker game.

biweekly/bimonthly

The prefix *bi* means *two* or *twice*, as in *bifocals* or *binational*. But when used with terms of duration (weekly, monthly, yearly), its definition has split into contradictory meanings; *biweekly* can mean either twice a week **or** every two weeks.

If you must use *bi* with these terms, restrict it to refer to every two weeks, months or years (except in *biannual*, which **must** mean semiannual). But you'll do better to avoid *bi* completely. You can get by very well with the prefix *semi*, which means "occurring twice within a period"; a semimonthly payment is made twice each month. For the other sense of *bi*, use explicit language: *Once every two months; every other year*. These expressions are like Volvos: they're bulky but reliable, and will get your readers where you want them to go.

capital/capitol

Capital refers to a seat of government (London, *capital* of England), upper-case letters (a *capital* P), the uppermost part of an architectural column, or a crime punishable by death. *Capitol* means only one thing—the building or buildings in which a legislature meets.

complement/compliment

A *complement* fills up, completes or makes perfect, while a compliment is an expression of respect or admiration.

- The young director was an ideal *complement* to the aging board.
- His appointment at such a young age deserves *compliment*.

council/consul/counsel

A *council* is a group of people who serve in a legal, administrative, or advisory capacity. The other two words, when used as nouns, refer to individuals; a *counsel* is a legal advisor (or the advice the advisor gives you); a *consul* represents a government in foreign countries. Of the three sound-alikes, only *counsel* works as a verb—to give advice.

His lawyer *counseled* him to see the *consul* for help in replacing his visa.

continual/continuous

These two are trouble even for the pros. As the dictionary definitions overlap, follow common usage as your guide. *Continual* means repeated often, while *continuous* means without a stop.

- He was *continually* awakened by the firecrackers.
- The rain fell *continuously* for three days, flooding the entire plain.

disinterested/uninterested

A *disinterested* observer is impartial; an *uninterested* person just doesn't care. They have long been interchanged, with marginal acceptability. If you use either one, make sure your context is clear.

- The lawyer feared it would be impossible to find a *disinterested* jury.
- The bailiff yawned; he was utterly *uninterested* in the case.

flaunt/flout

To *flaunt* is to display obviously, to make a show of; to *flout* is to defy with contempt or mockery.

- The senator *flaunted* his affair with the glamorous lobbyist.

- The senator *flouted* the law by shredding records of his campaign contributions.

gamut/gauntlet
When you run the *gamut* (of emotions, for example), you pass through a full range. To run a *gauntlet* is less pleasant; the word derives from the old military punishment, in which the accused was forced to run between two lines of men who struck him with sticks or other weapons. In modern usage, a *gauntlet* can refer to any ordeal.

hopefully
When used properly, *hopefully* means just what it says: full of hope. In loose modern usage, however, hopefully has broadened to express the hope of the *writer*, rather than of the subject modified by this adverb.

Proper:	The boy rose hopefully to his feet, sensing his beating was over.
Modern:	Hopefully, the rain will soon be over.

In discriminating circles this second usage remains taboo, and brands its author as an amateur.

however

When used to mean nevertheless, *however* rests more comfortably in the middle of a sentence, rather than at the start.

> Awkward: *However*, we resumed full speed after the damaged car was towed.
>
> Improved: We resumed full speed, *however*, after the damaged car was towed.

However can begin a sentence when it means "in whatever way" or "to whatever extent."

- *However* the wind blows, the ship will still lose the race.
- *However* long the odds, she never stopped trying.

immigrate/emigrate

These two are mirror opposites. To *emigrate* is to leave your country of birth; to *immigrate* is to enter a new country. Emigrants inevitably become immigrants, whether legal or illegal.

imply/infer

Another pair of mirror words, these two are widely mistaken for one another. To *imply* is to hint, or suggest, or indicate without saying directly; to *infer* is to conclude from the facts—or from another's implication.

- He *implied* that the new boss would be difficult for us to work with.
- I *inferred* that my job would become less pleasant.

in regard to/as regards

Either can be used to mean *concerning*, or *with respect to*. But *in regards to* is simply wrong.

lay/lie

Of all the verbs, these two are probably most vexing to the average writer. The distinction is actually quite logical, despite the similarity in sound. *Lay* (principal parts *lay, laid, laid, laying*) is a **transitive verb**; that is, it always takes a direct object.

- He *laid* his cards on the table: a royal flush.
- *Lay* your weary head down to rest. (Present tense.)

Lie (principal parts lie, lay, lain, lying) is an **intransitive verb**—a self-contained action with no direct object.

- We loved to *lie* on the beach for hours.
- We *lay* in bed until noon. (Past tense.)

loan/lend
Your high-school English teacher was wrong; *loan* can be used as a verb (as a substitute for *lend*), and has been for centuries. It is most appropriate in financial or commercial contexts. *Lend* is preferred for more general transactions.

- The mortgage banker *loaned* them the money without a credit check.
- My neighbor *lent* me his lawnmower last week.

oral/verbal
Oral is the more restrictive, as it applies only to spoken words; a *verbal* agreement can be made either in writing or in conversation. To avoid mis-understanding, replace *verbal* with either *spoken* or *written*, as appropriate.

practical/practicable
To be *practical* is a positive virtue; it means that you rely on things of proven usefulness and value. *Practicable* applies not to a person, but to a plan or project that is deemed workable.

- A *practical* woman, she put her odd dollars in mutual funds.

- The scheme seemed *practicable* until it came time to put it into action.

provided/providing
One qualifies, the other gives freely.

- The reorganization plan will work, *provided* the unions accept a wage freeze.
- The unions voted their assent, *providing* the president with critical support.

regretful/regrettable
Like hopeful, *regretful* modifies its subject. Writers who wish to inject their own regret must use *regrettable*.

- She was *regretful* to have missed the dinner party.
- *Regrettably*, the game was suspended by a downpour.

respectfully/respectively
The first shows respect or honor; the second refers to items taken in order.

- He answered his boss firmly but *respectfully*.
- He and I were voted secretary and treasurer, *respectively*.

shall/will

In traditional usage, *shall* expressed future action in the first person ("I *shall* go to the office"), while *will* was used only for the second and third persons. To supply emphasis, the rules were reversed.

- You *shall* obey my every order!
- I *will* not be denied my rightful inheritance.

In modern usage, however, *will* is acceptable whenever it sounds natural. *Shall* remains useful to suggest formality or politeness.

Shall we get together this evening?

that/which

While the rule is not as strict as it used to be, it's still best to use *that* to introduce a "defining" clause, and *which* to connect a "commenting" clause.

- The hamburger chain, *which* was best known on the East Coast, is now going national.
- A company *that* diversifies is more likely to prosper.